Online Arbitrage For Beginners:

How to Source, Buy, Resell Items Online and Make Money

By

Dale Blake

Table of Contents

Introduction 5

Chapter 1. Arbitrage Concept 6

Chapter 2. How to Apply Arbitrage on The Internet (Online Arbitrage) 8

Chapter 3. Different Types of Online Arbitrage 10

Chapter 4. Understanding Your Market 14

Chapter 5. Sourcing Your Items 18

Chapter 6. Where to Find Your Desired Items 21

Chapter 7. Crosschecking Your Item – The Good Versus Bad Checklist 25

Chapter 8. Understanding The Pricing 28

Conclusion 30

Thank You Page 31

Online Arbitrage For Beginners: How to Source, Buy, Resell Items Online and Make Money

By Dale Blake

© Copyright 2015 Dale Blake

Reproduction or translation of any part of this work beyond that permitted by section 107 or 108 of the 1976 United States Copyright Act without permission of the copyright owner is unlawful. Requests for permission or further information should be addressed to the author.

This publication is designed to provide accurate and authoritative information in regard to the subject matter covered. This work is sold with the understanding that the publisher is not engaged in rendering legal, accounting, or other professional services. If legal advice or other expert assistance is required, the services of a competent professional person should be sought.

First Published, 2015

Printed in the United States of America

Introduction

With internet penetration and speeds getting better by the day, more and more people are taking their life online. Even though the most notable adoption of the internet could be on the social media and general blogging world, there is a raising juggernaut in online shopping. As online transaction channels become more secure, merchants are leveraging this opportunity to bring goods and sometimes services to consumers who are not willing to walk around looking for a physical store.

While this online retail business has been around for a while, a more lucrative option that works on the arbitrage concept lurks behind the normal retail business. Arbitrage, in its simplest form, is all about buying goods at a cheaper market and selling them at a more expensive market. With the internet making things so simple, you could implement the concept of online arbitrage and make profits off goods that need not be in your warehouse in the first place.

Chapter 1. Arbitrage Concept

Let us suppose that for some reason, an online curio shop in Africa is selling a mahogany giraffe sculpture at $10 dollars. On eBay, the same item is going at $200. It would make a financial sense to buy the item and sell it on eBay since you will make a profit. This is arbitrage at its simplest.

Even though it could sound as a little offset in prices is all you need to get the business going, there are a couple of factors to consider before venturing into arbitrage. You must take it as a conventional production business. Factor in the time and money you would put into acquiring an item and finally delivering it to the client. In this case, for instance, while you could purchase the giraffe for $10, you might have to use $100 in shipping and handling. Your profit, in this case, would be $90 and not the whooping $190 you had in mind.

Arbitrage, therefore, is encompasses both the asset's cost and the effort expended in acquiring it. Creating a perfect balance between these two will ensure that you get the right profit. After all, only the profit margin that matters when it comes to online arbitrage.

Chapter 2. How to Apply Arbitrage on The Internet (Online Arbitrage)

With the internet bringing everything onto your fingertips, arbitrage has evolved into a more powerful business that could earn you profits and a luxurious income. However, with most of the information out there, the competition tends to be stiffer. Applying the simple concept of buying in one play, for instance eBay and selling on another, for instance Craigslist is to simple a plan to work. You need to be at the top of your game, to stay ahead of your competitors.

Taking on the tenacity and dynamicity of the internet and using it to your advantage would be the most viable way out of this. Even though there are a couple of tools that will help you make online commodity comparisons, investing some time into doing it on your own research will give you the edge.

Think about it. A better part of your competitors will be using these tools. This means everyone will try to arbitrate the same thing. In this case, it will be all about whoever makes it to the market first and makes a kill before competitors flood the market. Doing the search on your own, however, increases your chances of latching on unique items that will give you a better edge.

Moreover, understanding that online arbitrage is not limited to online offers will make you leverage local stores selling goods cheaply. If your local collector can sell you NFL jerseys at a price cheaper than what you see on eBay, why not move in for the kill, make a bulk purchase and take the jerseys online.

Implementing a hybrid approach will help give you a better profit margin on the online arbitrage market. Acting quickly and decisively will ensure that you 'strike the iron as it glows.'

Chapter 3. Different Types of Online Arbitrage

EBAY Arbitrage

Online arbitrate is common in EBay. Buyers take advantage of inexperienced sellers and get products at low prices. This is possible because of various reasons including:

Inexperienced sellers who list their products in inappropriate categories with lower demand. Desperate sellers end up listing their products in wrong categories thus attracting lower pricing than what is averagely being offered in the market.

Incorrect product titles and descriptions by careless sellers, which in turn decreases visibility in EBAY, search engines.

Misspellings in listing titles. This can happen unintentionally because of poor English skills or failure to countercheck before submitting. It could also occur intentionally where sellers choose to submit misspelled titles because they ran out of space. While you may think abbreviations will work you are unwittingly sending your items to the doldrums of eBay.

Poor images. Valuable items can remain stagnant without any bids just because you posted very poor pictures. Dull and grainy photography do no justice to the value of a product and may instead turn potential buyers away.

OPTIONS Arbitrage

It involves both buying and selling of options within a similar exchange or in different exchanges. This has to happen simultaneously. It involves domestic and foreign exchanges where one has not adjusted its options pricing for the currencies that are constantly changing their rates. Retail traders are advised against this strategy, as it is more suited for exchange ground traders because they can accommodate price discrepancies within no time.

PPC Arbitrage with CPA network

Comparatively this is the best strategy. It has a bigger price difference between PPC and CPA. With well-done landing pages, traders are likely to appreciate the offers n CPA networks.

Sports Betting Arbitrage

This involves taking advantage of the odds errors that are given by two bookmarkers concerning a similar outcome. Arbitrage is applied on odds with only two outcomes. Price differences are what allow bettors to gain from their outcome. Though once famous, improved technology continues to make this type of arbitrage rare. It is not possible to control breach of human weaknesses using well-designed software thus disadvantaging others when it comes to giving odds.

AdSense Arbitrage

One of the most popular arbitrage strategies a few years back. Entrepreneurs to take advantage of price difference between advertising keywords in AdWords and AdSense use it. The ads direct any person clicking on them to a website that is optimized for keywords that are more expensive. Its popularity continues to decrease due to Google's crackdown on its practice online. It involves bidding for the lowest priced AdWords while at the same time directing visitors to pricy AdSense. It is also allowed to use search engine paid traffic so long as the AdWord remains lower in price than the AdSense.

This strategy is more risky as there is no clue as to how much Google will pay for the AdSense in addition, it is not a guarantee that even when directed, visitors will always click on the AdSense.

Chapter 4. Understanding Your Market

Market size potential

It is advisable to choose a market niche and products with small market sizes. Too small market niches have low keyword searches. The problem with narrowing a market niche is the extra expense you will have to incur getting the target customers as well as hindering your potential for growth. You are better off defining your audience but not going into the details of likes and dislikes. A good product for example will be one that caters for a specific group, say pregnant women between the ages of 25 and 40 and not one that targets the same group of pregnant women with a specific liking.

Fad, trend, or growing

It is mandatory to know where your product stands in the market. Categorize the product either as falling in the trending, fad or growing market categories. Use tools such as Google trend to find out when it is most profitable to sell a product since timing is very important too. You are likely to get a clear picture of whether your product is trending, fad or stable in the market. Any important pointers should trigger further research that will in turn help you to know the possible cause of the problem.

Your target customer

While getting into extreme customer details may not be necessary, you have to know the type of audience you want to reach as well as their potential of purchasing products online. Depending on the age group that your product targets, certain factors will play out. Teens may not be able to buy your products online, because they do not have credit cards making this an important factor to consider. The other example could be that of a product that targets a group of customers with low technology and e-commerce adoption levels. To be successful, you will have to adjust your online store to accommodate these individuals especially if they are your primary clients.

Competition

Consider your product's competition landscape. You need to know if you have a large competition, small competition or no competition at all. A niche with many key players indicates market validation and you may have to do something different to attract and retain customers in the already established market. Customers here know about existing products and will need convincing to turn and adopt your product. Work on creating a good customer attention and building market share.

This is the general rule of competition. The simplest way to turning it round lies in using lesser prices or giving some purchase incentives. If you have a trick that will give you an upper hand in the competition, then you can safely move into that market. If you don't, it is an indicator that you should look for some other product to sell.

Local availability of the product

You are likely to have a more difficult time selling a product online whose substitutes are available locally. No one will waste time ordering a product online when he or she can get one that is as effective in a local store nearby. The important thing is to differentiate your products and stand out. This way, you may be able to convince people to look online for your product. Ensure that you have a way of giving them better quality, better price and a range of selections of the product. Customers may be difficult to convince but once you get it right you have yourself a loyal following.

Chapter 5. Sourcing Your Items

The most common form of arbitrage on eBay involves sellers raking garage and flea sales of valuable goods. In most cases, the yard seller does not understand the true value of whatever he or she is selling. They would most definitely have undervalued the commodity. Applying this concept to pure online arbitrage is a little bit trickier. You will have to keep a constant eye for such online sales and capitalize as soon as you can.

The core problem, however, is knowing what to buy and not where to buy it. The fact that a rare game DVD sells at $25 on Craigslist and $20 on eBay is not guarantee that the prices will remain so for the next couple of hours, let alone day. The profit margin, therefore, is never the answer to determining what items you should arbitrate.

Unique

The first thing to consider when looking for your items is their uniqueness. If something is unique and hard to come by at an affordable price, chances are that you will sell all your units before the market prices take a plunge. Choose a couple of niches and dedicated yourself to understanding its unique yet valuable items that you can lay your hands on. This should be your gate pass to an impressive online arbitration kill.

Wieldy

Wield deals with how fast you can shuttle the item from your seller and deliver it to your next customer. Virtual items like subscriptions and ebooks would be the wieldiest. The African mahogany giraffe sculpture, on the other hand, would be cumbersome unless you have the right importation connection. Striking a balance between the profit and the ease of handling the item is key to running a successful arbitrage business as a beginner.

Good quality

Even though you are selling cheap, you do not have any reason to sell people substandard commodities. This will destroy your online merchant reputation and make any future sells next to impossible. Take time to ascertain the quality of the commodity you choose to sell before taking your deal live.

A Product Versus a Niche

Very few arbitrage experts ever report of success by working in a niche unless they are really big companies. A niche is too wide. You might not have the money or labor to supply all the niche needs. The most sensible way out lies in identifying that single product that you can easily sell at a profit. Searching for niche products pits you against so much data. Not only with your efforts scatter over a wider area but also leave you lesser room to move in for single commodity kills whenever the opportunity presents itself.

It doesn't matter whether you are interested in expanding or not. You have to identify something that will work for you, something that will be your flagship product. By focusing on a single commodity, you stand a better chance at staying up to date with its trends and any variations or alternatives that are on demand.

Chapter 6. Where to Find Your Desired Items

Once you have an idea of what you will be selling, it is now time to identify the market you will buy them from you. As we have already established, you have two options:

- An online search

- An offline purchase

Online Search

This could by far be your simplest option. All you might need to do this search is internet connection a PC and perhaps a mug of coffee. At this point, I presume that you will have an idea of trending commodities that you believe you can sell at a profit. If you don't, this section could also help you identify the best deals to include in your catalogue.

Begin with a simple Google search including what you want to sell followed by the magic word 'sale.' This is a good start if you have no idea what sites to search in. Moreover, it will give you a list of even the small individual sellers on the internet that have the commodity you are searching for on sale.

Alternatively, you could do a comparison on the top online merchant sites like eBay, Shopify, Craigslist and Amazon. The only problem with these sites is the deals over here go really fast. Your fellow arbitrage masters know these hunting grounds as the back of their palms. They will pounce on most deals before they can last a day.

However, by using the right monitoring and comparison tools, you can always identify deals as soon as they go live. Comparison tools come in the form of browser add-ons or sometimes complete websites. The add-ons will give a notification once a commodity in a niche you selected shows a tangible price difference in two market niches. Website tools only work when you are using them in person. If you are adept enough, you can easily identify deals and closing in before the others swoop in for the kill.

A general Google search (Google is the most famous but you can use any other search engine you fancy), on the other hand, will give you a wide array of online shops with lucrative deals. The rule of the thumb is if the shop has an amazing deal on an electric kettle, it most definitely will have good deals on other commodities. It is up to you to peruse through the catalogues and make the right decisions.

Offline Purchases

While online purchase are simpler as they do not require you to move around, they can rarely beat offline purchases. In most cases, you will be dealing with someone who got the commodities from an offline supplier. You will be dealing with a middleman. Eliminating this link in the chain will not only plug you into a good supply line but also increase your profit margin.

Identifying your destinations for these offline purchases can remain online based. A good example we had at the start was about a mahogany giraffe from Africa that was selling for $10. If you can travel to Africa, buy a couple of them from the real producers, chances are that you will cut some slack off the cost.

This, however, would not be needed if you are dealing with virtual goods like tickets or stocks. The beauty of arbitrating on soft goods is that you do not have to worry about the shipping delays or do the delivery logistics once someone places an order. Sometimes, if you do not have enough resources or time to move around, soft arbitrating would be the most viable idea.

Examples of things you could deal with in this process ranges from stocks, to advertising slots in AdSense or even reselling important game tickets. Arbitration is all about selling something whose price varied from one market to another. If you can lay your hands on such a thing in a legal way, then this should be your key to sealing your deal of a lifetime.

This is the theory behind every offline purchase. You will have a better shot at getting something that you want without the interference of a middle man. After all, you want to be the middleman, the shouldn't be many people between you and the real producer of the commodity in question.

Chapter 7. Crosschecking Your Item – The Good Versus Bad Checklist

Good products

A good product should be able to get you a good profit margin. In this case we are talking selling the product for twice its buying price. Anything less than that will be strenuous on your part. It should be able to pay off if you are to keep your business afloat. While sometimes doing with less than the double profit sounds good enough, arbitrage only works perfectly when we are talking of 100+ percent profit. The boom won't last long and you have to be in a position to make the kill as it lasts.

The product should have a high demand which guarantees consistent buyers. It also has to be a product that can be sold all year round. You want something that will keep you on toes regardless of the season. Items such as Christmas cards only come around every 365 days. You will not possibly be spending the rest of the 364 days waiting for a one-day sale.

The products should be portable enough for you to carry around without seeking help. During shipment, weight of the cargo is usually what determines the prize charged for the goods. You will also have to incur storage costs until when you find transportation means. You may want to cut down on such costs.

Select unique products. Find a niche in the market and exploit it. It would be easier to market a unique product than going with the masses. Breaking into the industry would be easy if you have a product that is unique since it will intrigue consumers.

Products within a price range of $10 to $100 would be a better bet. However, it would need some bit of sacrifice to raise the large capital required. Products under $10 are worse off because of not only low profit margins but you will also be up against big importers. The difference being that they have the financial muscle while you don't.

Bad products

Products that have a trade mark on them will earn you a date at the attorney's office and not profit. Avoid them like a plague. It is not a risk you are willing to take especially when you are just starting off. You will not go further than the second step. If you are established, it is even worse because all your gains will be reduced to nothing.

For all it's worth, do not even give fragile products a second thought. You will not only have to deal with a lot of shipping requirements which translate to more cash you have to part with but it is just too risky.

Products offered by large organizations that have almost monopolized the market are just a bad idea. Chances that you will be able to penetrate such a market are close to zero. You will not be able to import as much as he does and furthermore, he is selling large volumes of the product. Uniqueness and consistency in sales should be you driving factor.

Products with great warranties and have high quality standard demands will give you nothing but constant headache. It is problematic enough that you have to handle the tedious shipment exercise. Adding these demands to the picture is recipe for trouble. There are better products that bring great returns and do not come with too much baggage.

Chapter 8. Understanding The Pricing

The viability of your product in the sale is dictated by its different pricing determinants. This could be loosely referred to as the markup. Selling things online comes with a great number of additional costs. There are the custom duty taxes, shipping costs, shopping cart costs and the time the merchant spends processing the order. All these have to be paid for. With an elaborate markup, you will not only know the costs to expect on the way should you decide to go on with the sell but also know when to pull off a given deal.

We could do our example using the Giraffe carving from Africa but we already decided that would be too bulky for beginners. Let us work with some super cheap iPhone 6 cases I found at Alibaba. The cost of manufacturing a single unit by the producer is $0.5 Packaging these units and shipping them to my location would take $50 for 1000 cases. This is also the minimum number of cases I can offer. The processing costs of the entire package total up to $20 and the VAT is $15. The total expenses of purchasing and shipping the whole package would be $585.

This translates to a cost of $0.585 per iPhone case. With the market I intent to sell to having cases at an entrance price of $1.2, I can easily sell my cases at double the price and still remain in the market. However, to be the best deal, I will have to lower my cost by a cent or two. This will cut down my profit from 100 percent to something close to 90 percent. This could be viable but it is always advisable to go for something that gives you a very wide profit margin.

Doing a complete pricing comparison before choosing on the commodity to arbitrate is crucial. Moreover, you have to ensure that you actually take the product through the entire purchase cycle without checking out to identify all the involved costs. In addition to this, you also have to pay attention to the minimum purchase clause. This will not only affect how much you invest into the product but also determine how good your resell logistics ought to be.

Conclusion

So many things can go into your arbitrage cart. Choosing your product wisely will determine the difference between you and your competitors. It is therefore paramount that you take time and do elaborate research before making your initial entry into the market.

Online arbitrage is highly dynamic. What was a hit a few days ago could easily be useless today. People will always get wind of the trick to supplying cheap, or the increase in supply will fuel market changes hence pushing the prices down. Moving fast and making the kill long before the bubble bursts would be one of the wisest ways to doing online arbitrage.

Thank You Page

I want to personally thank you for reading my book. I hope you found information in this book useful and I would be very grateful if you could leave your honest review about this book. I certainly want to thank you in advance for doing this.

If you have the time, you can check my other books too.

www.ingramcontent.com/pod-product-compliance
Lightning Source LLC
LaVergne TN
LVHW021747060526
838200LV00052B/3519